Waiting for Word

poems by

A. Jay Adler

Finishing Line Press
Georgetown, Kentucky

Waiting for Word

For Julia
True north and constant star

If something takes too long, something happens to you. You become all and only the thing you want and nothing else, for you have paid too much for it, too much in wanting and too much in waiting and too much in getting.
–Robert Penn Warren, All the Kings Men

Copyright © 2021 by A. Jay Adler
ISBN 978-1-64662-466-9 First Edition
All rights reserved under International and Pan-American Copyright Conventions. No part of this book may be reproduced in any manner whatsoever without written permission from the publisher, except in the case of brief quotations embodied in critical articles and reviews.

ACKNOWLEDGMENTS

"La Habana Nueva" in *Poetry Bay*
"What I'm Drinking These Days" in *Eclipse*
"Lives of the Poet" and "weightless" in *Adagio Verse Quarterly*
"Interstate" in the *Pebble Lake Review*
"Things in Themselves" in the *Pebble Lake Review*
"A Stone in Water" in the *Tipton Poetry Journal*
"Myth" in *Blood Lotus*
"Ocean's End," "A Lexicology of the Middle Years" and "The World Again in West Magazine
"The Twentieth Century Passes," "Place (traveling)," "The Cemeteries at Père-Lachaise and Montparnasse," and "Universal Art Gallery (Opening soon)," in *Footnote: A Literary Journal of History*
"The Living and the Dead" in the CUNY Center for the Humanities' *Light Relief from Lost and Found*

Publisher: Leah Huete de Maines
Editor: Christen Kincaid
Cover Art: Julia Dean
Author Photo: Julia Dean
Cover Design: Elizabeth Maines McCleavy

Printed in the USA on acid-free paper.
Order online: www.finishinglinepress.com
also available on amazon.com

Author inquiries and mail orders:
Finishing Line Press
P. O. Box 1626
Georgetown, Kentucky 40324
U. S. A.

Table of Contents

The World Again 1

The Words 2

Backstroke 4

Interstate 5

Lives of the Poet 6

A Lexicology of the Middle Years 7

What I'm Drinking These Days 8

Things in Themselves 9

Myth 10

Place (traveling) 11

The Twentieth Century Passes 12

A Geology of Birds 14

The Living and the Dead 15

La Habana Nueva 16

"Universal Art Gallery" (Opening soon) 18

The Cemeteries at Père-Lachaise and Montparnasse 20

Impolitic Manifesto 22

The Last Word 24

Gravity 25

Weightless 27

Full Flush 28

Ocean's End 29

Infinite Nocturne 31

If I Were You 32

Ringolevio 33

A Stone in Water 35

There Being 36

The World Again

darkness come to light Bright son
sitting in a pool, calm, ripple, feel Grass
around Pain of becoming Oh Tall faces
against the wide sky so Hold me Hear
me not Cry in silence Where I come
from In this utter presence From this
merely mine With these great and meager
presents Shine

The Words

What at first came easy,
   in the end turned hard; and what so readily flowed,
      too rarely formed.

      (When there is no word for it
      when word has not come,)

The tributary lives I led
   —island distances horizoned like shimmery lures—
      instead in late light largely loom

      (of mouth or eaten, or for want
      of a better, so they stick in your throat,)

as dry salvages on which I wrecked.
   Thought I'd plant myself, bloom libraries
      of lives I'd write to live,

      (then mark my word, they'll
      all fail, the first and the last,)

but only ocean crags,
   I caught and hung their faces, leapt to passing steamers,
      sailed on them singing,

      (because no one sent or left
      either the good one or as good as my.)

til they sank beneath
   the slapstick straits of time, a squandering of purpose
      that lost its purpose in the maelstrom.

      (And even if you finally get one in,
      before or after you break it,)

Looking back,
   peering forward, I wonder, what were you thinking writing,
      not writing, or thinking you were?

      (don't put them in my mouth
      if they're empty or beyond them.)

You spilled them across the floors
uncollected, scattered them from windows without
wind to bear them earward,

(Are they merely words, that someone
always leaves or gives one, spreads one)

swallowed them like bees:
yellowjackets of angry ferment, bumbles of busyness
sailing long lazy loops

(—of mouth and to the wise—
that I was at a loss for? In a word,)

among the marigold and mallow.
Lodged there. Lay there. Till I die or they do,
some choking, stingless death.

(what's the word? Mum's it, maybe.
Or in other words, take my word,

borne out of the buzzing hive,
deep dark and honeyed down the fervent center where
I was born, to bear the words

into this bare barkless
leaving and unleaving left to go. Write them, then. Be them.
Of all the world's words, deliver

this one, then that:
world the word departing, and worlding word, word the world
in enunciation of our parting.

Backstroke

In retrospect
one swings the arm
no, flings the hand
the arm trailing
like an
unforeseen consequence.
The feet paddle
frantic ducklings far from shore.
Done right, the center is still
fixed in travel
while mill-winding motion
foot-flapped propulsion
over the calm plane provide
sheer glide.
The Uncertain
glance over the shoulder at
what lies ahead.
That far? So soon?
But, then, rhythm is lost.
The extra effort exhausts.
Better, not. We'll know
when we get there.
Straight ahead, behind
what prompts us persists—
push off and kick—
but pales, too, a rippling gleam
we leave in the wake
stroke after stroke
a long departing gaze
reaching to arrive.
In this start to
finish, skimming
the glassy surface of dreams
we know where we come from:
the point remains. Swimmers recede.

Interstate

To swerve is to miss
To miss to long for:
A receding highway light
In the middle of the country
Through the center of the night.

How distance beckons and turns away.

This starry billboard rises
Along the road, through every county
It chances one may go.

To miss is to fail
To reach or contact. The tire
Misses the road. In the general vagueness

In the general night, the rest stops
Blink and sigh over cup and saucer
Above the glum Formica—
The accidental faces.

The windows mirror the way.

A stretch of darkness, like longing's light
How far I must have traveled
When you rise up quickly, surely
It's always the center of the road
And I swerve and miss you, miss you.

Lives of the Poet

I see them all

succumb to the electric choke of the coffee drip
the dogs at my feet moan for the bone
this tenor's lyric flight
lands on the baseboard dust
a wash of light in the afternoon's
hushed diminuendo
at the sink before me
and I, in the end-day yard through the window
journey back across this bounded place
to my only fleeting self.

A Lexicology of the Middle Years

Tracing the form of the last thing she says to me
how the lips round like ohs
sound bounds from bottom to top—
cavernous cry of the bone—
digging etymology
out of anger, the origin of the flip
concluding word, the yet unspoken
plea for kindness
seeking in my vocabulary
some cognate for this long transmission
of intimacy, still I think:
I have no ear for the young words
all buff and shiny, and not a thing to say at the bar.
Let me hear them spoken around the block
a time or two, their vowels longing for consonance
what gives them meaning—prefix of desire
suffix of regret—inflected now only by time
the history of their enunciation deeper
than any beginning I can know.

What I'm Drinking These Days

None of that will do
                I said.
One hundred proof, unvarnished.
Tear the roof right out of your mouth
Just to speak it. Sizzle the synapses
Just to think it. Burn a hole in your
Rot gut so bad the body'll quiver
Like seizure, the arms flap a
Pump and jerk, like one of those
Old mountain moonshiners who swigged it
Long and deep, danced a square, a hoot and a holler
      Just to live with it.

It's hard to say when the body first fails the mind—
Constitution crawls at the feet of conviction
But water, I find, makes a delicate addition to
Cocktails and confession; liberates, they say
The robust bouquet
Of a biting but closed condition.
And ice, oh, that's nice for the chill of relief
From the molten lava you're serving.
I'll sit by the window. I'll glow in the sunset.
I'll savor the truth of my youth.
Don't share what you're thinking. I'm drinking.

Things in Themselves

A chair on a porch, unrocked
beneath the eaves, the uncollected
leaves in flat November light—
a car parked keyless beside the road.

The windless world blows, a clock tick stuck.
Still, the guttered ball waits. The absent shingle
recalls the roof, never falling but always
fell. Below, something grounded.

Middle of a lot, a stone that dropped, or was:
some young or murderous hand in flight
yesterday or when a hominid loped from view.
It lies among the weeds, mirthless, unbloodied

but so presented to the chair, so equal
to the leaves, far relative to the car.
Then a bud pushes relentless petals against the tock
And a shadow passes over the clock.

Myth

Barreled over some wheels on the 66, out West
breaching the old wind, earth's unending hail of dust
flaring into fire glow in the light of the world's round rim
it isn't theory now—desire incommensurate
with its condition. So far from home, the now
alien beginning, measuring the progress
of Venus against the millipede's march
it is what you do, or daily do, dare to do:
crack a word against an empty instant, crack another—
shouts in the wind-rush—so you can barrel through
as if it isn't so, as if it is.

Place
traveling

It's a road, behind and before. I wander it like dust
with wind for a will.

Arizona, now, ranges over mountain and pass
desert brush and Geronimo's ghost for, once
a watchful youth

while Los Angeles is leaving, spinner and lure
for a hungry eye, hooked, but never caught.
They're soft winds over those ocean dreams. They blow
they blow.

Soon Oklahoma, the South, Virginia
Michigan, the Northern Plains: the sweep and particular
of country and tale—also a vision. Deep breath and sigh, wide-eyed
I have seen this meadow, that rock, timber of a home long ago
I had always imagined.

Budapest, too, and Buenos Aires, and Asian jungle
whose river snakes to a mountain source, the hidden life
from early springs. Sought a seed, too, where my father
sprang from Galicia, a cold and foreign soil in which to germinate
a Jew. How far, then, back to ramble home? Be gusted over Sinai sands?
Gather in the Great Rift Valley?

Where I come from, every feeling calls a name, every
name a habitation, a place of birth, and all my destinations merge
into me. When the Dutch first spied Manhattan's breast, and paid
with all the rich corruptions of the heart for every generation crossing
Brooklyn Ferry, they opened up a harbor, carried human cargo
the city still unloads. Hudson wandered, too, up Mahicanittuk River
and never arrived beyond it.

The Twentieth Century Passes
for my mother and father

1.

There is no way to know where she lost it
—along the way, or where the concrete
steps reminded her that nothing belongs to us anyway
not even ourselves. Her father worked a kiosk
on Second Avenue and Eighth Street
green and shuttered at night
like the sleeping world
all its wondrous and awful news now
old and locked away.
He sold many Jewish papers: The Daily Forward,
which they moved in the slow procession,
stories unreported by time.
She has told me this
many times, but for the first time (always, for her)
only since the earth rose up
to meet her from the drive of Lawry's restaurant.
She can still smell
at the threshold of the doorway
under the stoop on fourth street
the odor of an unfavored child (who married when she could)
though she cannot place it anymore.
We eat our sandwiches.
"Did you like tuna?" she asks, as if puzzling the mysteries.
I nod: "It was my favorite."
At that, we both turn to Katherine Hepburn, sixty years ago
and taut as a bowstring, wonder if the stars remember
every escapade and kiss, or if sometimes in the darkness
they sit and only stare
at some actor on the screen.

2.

The way his hand trembles a little
reaching with the key to unlock
the lock that opens
to his home again. How he cannot hear
the lips he cannot see

beside him. How in the spreading fog
through which he reaches he might see
a dirt road and a wagon passing,
a short, bearded and theological man
crossing in the wagon's traffic:
then fierce riders, with fast bridled fury
madly grinning at the bit, their cry and whinny
and his grandfather bleeding and bootless on the ground…

The key finds its home
in a century of terror
these are its chambers
its tumblers made to fit by some smith
of hidden craft.
There is simple business now:
a kettle to fill, the tea to brew
a piece of fish, some bread
a stretch of the long unyielding muscle that has tread
the mill from Orinin to Warsaw, Nairobi to Palestine
to gyms throughout New York and Woodland Hills.
Some curls and presses, too.
What weights are those to carry?
On the balcony, beside his dozing wife, in forgetfulness
he wills to happen, he sits and fills the distance without care.
Though he cannot see it, he knows
it is out there, and the salt sea Pacific
breathes clean in his nose.
This is the key, these
are the chambers
that tumbled in dreams in the night.
From hard beginnings sometimes
easy ends.

A Geology of Birds
(my parents, grown old)

Water has worn us, like more time's mountain
flow we could ever have seen coming
left us on this present bank like stones
found in near relation on the ground.
The inexorable flood rounds us
apart, our mineral origin
matter only for geologist's eyes.

Who would have thought
the birth cries, stone's cries
water forgot, we'd forget?
A mother's songs of deliverance drift
homeless in the burbling stream
a father's tillering hand lies idle
and ritual kisses
try to shape from lips
an early, pressing need
like the air we'd gasp for lack of.

But need
like the nested sparrow's
gaping mouth, wild with hunger
for the seed of all that follows
need departs, a winter's calling
and we fly, stones into birds
into another hemisphere
so far from any beginning
nearer even the youngest's end
riding currents we cannot name
feeling, as we seek what calls us
we see a wing we knew.

The Living and the Dead

To be a grandparent, to me, was to be unreal, to be dead
as the past in which the dead have passed,
un-near as nameless bodies, effaced, so disembodied,
disappeared before I lived. My face pressed
against the soiled pane of my mother's memory, light
could pass through the glass only from me:

through England and before-time, to turbulence
like boiling water, lines scored across the earth's pupil.
Map of seeing, cartography of disastrous forgetting,
the unsettled unremembered beyond the pale.
Her father, my mother said, worked a kiosk
on Second Avenue and 8th Street, the Lower East Side,
green and shuttered at night, when the living have fled
and the dead haunt the dark closets of your eyes.

Oaxaca and Huehuetenango, Tegucigalpa and San Salvador,
boiling waters. Call them history name them lives,
fragrant with steam of sweet or savory dumpling soups:
knaidelach, kreplach, chocoyotes. How does anyone
get to where they're going, to be found there showing
themselves as they are? *Zayde, Bubbe, Abuelo y Abuelita.*

A chair in a recess of a kiosk on Broadway, in the City of Angels
con su esposa talking the world. Coming and going
those who stop in their showing, grey heads blent with the sun.
When it rises and lights them, through slats at my window,
I peer. Passing through glass, in my time, before-time appears.
Water boils in the kitchen, and no sign of *mi abuela* for a week.

La Habana Nueva

In the new Havana
which is the old Havana
but older, as Dylan was younger than that now
Cesar—one eye now forever lost and spinning
in centerfield, glove and bare hand waiting and reaching
calmly beseeching the sky for the ball—
used to play for *Industriale*
who are the Yankee invasion that took.
When he sees your eyes search the cathartic
saline sick facades, as his eye
still seeks high drives
he says, "Where you from?" and you say
Estados Unidos, and he says "*Estados Unidos!*
Ah, my friend," and hugs you like the plate.
He tells you what went wrong—
"the sun, she was lost in the ball"—
and shows you *Granma*, a mother
of a boat. Then the promised beer
in the bar where no tourists go
sluggish and dark like the future
turns into richer rum, a dollar a shot
on you, and goes down center smooth
and warm, like patience on the tongue.
A few convertible pesos more, for the baby's milk
and his crazy eye catches your wallet
swollen with his desire, and you flee
a lover from too much need
ditch guilty cigarettes on the counter
because he wants your friendship
but your money more.

In the new Havana
where the sun is lost in the ball
everyone is dizzy and calm with waiting.
We live in this world
orisha of embargoed time, colonial place
salsa of soul, *danzon* of dreams
dos ambos mundos at the Caribbean mouth, singing
la trove of old world, orotund anthem of new.
In the slow hurricane of history
beating BONG-O onto shore, conga
into sugar cane commerce, tobacco leaf lore
nothing is swept away, everything sways

like the coconut palm in the tropical storm.
For God arrived, armored, in ships, belly
blown big by the world's westering wind
devoured the old in the new, the new in the gold
horizons and the beaches, white with time.
But everything stays, nothing sweeps away
completely the Taino from the long dry bone
of earth—can wax spurred heels from palacio floors—
or cleans the mouth of language
or sets fire to the memory
that houses those who fled
or emancipates the future
from the past.
During and after the great gulf gale
that blustered over battlements and fields
and beat a hail of coin upon the curling tongues
the Cuban waters swelled with change
but on this island nothing is washed away
what leaves it stays, everything sways
like the coconut palm in the tropical storm.

In the new Havana
everyone is loved
and no one is scorned by a weathered God.
A newer world rises like the *Malecón* spray
high over the seawall, soaking old Chevys
drenching the wounded pavement and the flesh
of dark lonely walkers, and Cesar is one.
He trawls in the wash for a light in the shadows
a dollar in a handshake, and the world's great room
in a dreamy conversation. But still he is loved
by Ché and Fidel, with a new world's ardor
and he's loved by his cousins in Miami
and New Jersey, too, in their passionate refusal.
In the new Havana everyone is loved
but orphaned of care.
They live in this world
orisha of embargoed time, colonial place
salsa of soul, *danzon* of dreams, slow
hurricane of history:
dos ambos mundos at the Caribbean mouth

                                            singing.

"Universal Art Gallery"
(Opening soon)

They hang themselves
long before some canvass gets stretched
between any two imaginations.
And the photographs
reproduce on their own, develop in place
ahead of a shuttering eye:
such images as no artist makes
but renders service to.

They claim all the cornered walls
of the large and airy space
take title of every geometry
frame themselves
as round and rolling hips like hills
horizontal in the grass
or envision beyond plain sight
the colors of a form
there is no shape to mold.
They insert themselves in flip bin copies
of an Adirondack lake
or replicate unnumbered
those anointed moments that might be us
in whoever's kissed or fallen figure
on one of those days we all remember.

They develop on a film
of organ tissue and self:
brain's brief charge against
the emulsion of experience.
The patrons cannot buy
these ephemera they capture
like themselves in the mirror;
they own them all in common.
In a continuum of sight
along a corridor of blank and wondrous faces
gargoyles grimace, soup cans jingle
and innocents flee themselves.

It's all a fire in the recess
of a spot in the back

down the stairs at the end
of a far, narrow hallway.

We stand there at angles
our eyes like white diamonds
and stare beneath a lifetime's
long and lurid, neon flicker.

The Cemeteries at Père-Lachaise and Montparnasse

Samuel Beckett waits the wasting changes here,
lies, to my surprise, in an earthly grave.
In what grave sense does he remain, then, and not go?
And Baudelaire is here, and Balzac, and Hugo:
all the flares that burst and flickered
embered into monuments of fame and stone.

Beauvoir shares the plot and stone with Sartre
though they would not split the rent and gas in life:
they have no need for their own space now
in the cold autonomy of the dark and silent.

A spare "MD" engraved in granite
marks the last *écriture de Duras,*
and where Morrison burned and crashed to rest
his fans leave lyrics that urge their human voice
to "break on through" to some other side.

And wild as Wilde lived his life
he's Wilder still in death: an unknown benefactress
restores his tomb, where scores of rosy lipstick lips
kiss in swirls of renewed delight
his latest marble monument.

They all appear where I least expect them
there in the solid ground, now
in the living light of an autumn day.
Tristan Tzara, just one letter in a random
alphabet along a shaded walk da da.
Man Ray, Seyrig, Sarah Bernhardt
in their quiet places, Simone Signoret
and Yves Montand in endless embrace again
die and depart and drift
into aging pages of repetition and renown
dwell among the sacred scenes and bookmarks in midnight light
—die and depart and reassert their natural selves
before each mortal, passing gaze
beside each set of scraping soles.

So their light lingers, headlights in a fog
but they leave their darkness, too

as if the spirit's voyage requires a body's anchor
or where might they be found, or how afraid to leave?
And Eugene Ionescu hopes that Christ awaits him.

Turn by turn, far corner by corner
I find them oddly still in the world of dreams and fears
and I save for the end Alfred Dreyfus
most unexpected, most lonely
farthest from any marker on a map.
Crooked aisle by aisle, angled row by row
I scan the names and lives, but the soldier is sentenced
unjustly again: I cannot find him.

The gnarled and bony-fingered branches
splay leafless against the drear October sky
and what is there and isn't there
hangs nowhere in the cemetery air.
It is Paris 2003, or 4 or 5
and there are the family come to visit
the unknown lover who stands alone
an open gate, the nearby traffic
the fresh and wilting bounty of Serge Gainsbourg's tributes
the mausolea, the hidden reaches
the statues and a child running
(Samuel Becket waiting)
a cold stone bench, the hand that writes
the blown leaf, the millipede
the shadows of them all.

Impolitic Manifesto
November 8, 2016

It isn't so much that words fail as fail to measure up,
not inadequate to a task, but incommensurable
to things. They line the shore like vacant houses, rise up
indistinct in the hills above. We sail by, thoughts calling out.

I don't think they hear us...

So all this mess, all about, offers no surprise.
Civilization's rough delivery, breech and botched, squat-
dropped in a field, carries on in cries, a cruel labor
in dumb design, of inconceivable conception.

Upon this rock, Plymouth, mouth plum of dreams...

Yet these dreams we share with each other ravish the vision
(nightmares ravage our eyes), till we take them
as the peopled world. Our bodies, sculpted of dust and water,
scrape clay pots out of sediment, scan the sky for radiant vapors.

And dogs still bark at the moon...

For the achievement, such as it was, bold as a bird
free on the wing, manifest in its power, exceptional
in its reach, haunted by guiltlessness, mined from membranous
mind, out of nothing, an idea

of the free, dignified and rightful citizen...

That was the meaning, the conveyance from then to now,
the import of what was imparted, not the thing,
but the making out of it: what was to be recalled
in remembrance, of what we meant to make of ourselves,

what, taken outright, might be earned, might be squandered...

What, then? That half concealed and still, tigers in the bush,
we stalk ourselves? As if tigers conceive a destiny, or commemorate
their kill—solemn and ceremonious—worship the carcass
on altars of tooth and claw, fan holy columns of flies

in spirals to the sky.

The thing is done, the lie told—the offending body stinks,
and no one will claim it. Disguised as history, the present
maligns the past, ventriloquizes virtue, mocks all meaning,
while the pretenders cry in protest, and dissemble every seeming:

"Who are you to tell me? Who is anyone to know?"

History does not commit itself. May it remember, as well as it
forgets, who put this fire to flame, the political mind and its claim
that conscience might survive in calculation. Here, then, are the princes
in which men trust, their hoarding of silver and gold,

and there is no end to their getting ...

My father, yours, said on this rock, I will teach you to be a man,
to live as man and woman in fair relation, to know a man,
and what is not a man, measure of all things. This wealth alone
I leave you. For we cannot know the end of what we do,

though what we do will end.

The Last Word

Last words have the gasp of death, something still
to be said something more, with one's last breath, the periodic
sentencing of life. Last words are one of those things
people are always trying to get in,
the crow of the ultimate pronouncement, the
completed argument, the final trump. That'll show 'em.
And then the shrinking away from the great
expenditure of energy, the air sucked out of the room
by the unarticulated, continuing, disagreement,
a flicked flame burning in the small space between us.
I'll say no more. The last word in fully equalized, sub-woofered and tweetered,
multiphonic surround sound home entertainment, in variably
scalable, cross platform, internet solutions and messaging clients for
home or office, large or small. State of the art.
A digital poet strains for the precise, inexpressible byte;
the cursive hand reaches for the mind in sight: the new last word
rises from ashes in the empty dawn, takes flight,
beats wings, batters the air with the current of our ideas
the shock of its birth in utterance, and in the clash of sounds
the rumble of their atomic contesting for space
and the music of their longing for home—the end
words become us, or we them. Who can tell? Who can
tell?

Gravity
(after Sharon Olds' "The Victims")

So much weight careens and barrels by
clanking freight cars rapid fire on the fly
yet the days stretch out a flat terrain of minutes, hours
and the long declining mountain pass winds ever lower
slower from where I came to where I'm bound.
That's what I see, since you ask, as I ogle my shoes
landed now on Bowery after Market Street and Beale.
I can't tell you what I feel, only
misery's a thing made friends with, really, as much as found
sad sorry pity'll run you to the ground
as well as any mix of Thunderbird and Crown.

You took it and took it so
you couldn't take any more
because love and family were easy ambitions, their justification
harder work. To be God's own handprint on each other's lives.
Disenchantment sprang from us like children
children like regret.
Obligation wore against our soles
with grinding forgetfulness.
My suits in the closet
hung like slaughter.
The Bombay Gin ran to dark water,
where my eyes, like embers, slipped with a hiss from view.
One thing happened. Then another.
Hard luck always offers a first hand
or maybe returns an invitation.
I don't know.
But soon it was gone. Gone so fast.
You couldn't take it anymore.

One day, I don't remember, after a fifth I'd polished pretty quick
I was scuttling across the soundless floor
with all the other bottom dwellers scavenging the muddy bed
and she passed, among the day trippers, the night fishers, the sailors of deep waters
buoyed more precariously than they know.
Or was she searching for me?
I listed to her fathomless face, her wavering salmon eye
watched undulant balls of gurgling liquid plaint float from her mouth
heard their muffled entreaties ping in the depths like sonar.

I stared in wonder: the rainbow film that was their wordless, bubbled skin.
I lifted my finger ... and then I didn't.

She looks for me now in her oldest dreams
hopes to find me there weightless and young
and she with her gull cries trailing long legs above the cresting waves.
But she learns in the shifting moan of night
there's more fall in the sky can ever be lofted back in flight.
Gravity's our law, and all momentum moves to the massive center.
And there's where she spies me, with all the rest
each hung suspended in the dark silent current
bobbing slowly in his single shaft of pain
drifting up, drifting down, passing sideways like fish
in the cold blue light that names us.

weightless

we would, in what passes, be light
as lifted burdens leave us when they go

we would that our greenhouse homes
glassy and round, cutless of corner, be
biospheres that ease us through
the hard vacuum
of all that outer space beyond

we would live
as if made to be here

our gardens grow
and that was last year in Provence
before Tuscany
when Lilith learned to fly
                              the boys
would be grown now   so tall
and full of promise if we'd had them
if we'd made
that rock our thing

but all our particle charm   is not
massive enough, the dark matter
nothing
you can count on
the darker energy
a flight from what weighs us down

alas   poor Camus
we do not always find
our burden again
but sometimes are drawn
from what holds us together
expand forever in infinite drift
the cold dim death of the farthest lights
so far from their brilliant creation
invisible and cheerless and slow

Full Flush
for Jerry "Jacket"

Full flush on the Avenue in your ja-quette and shades,
all leathered up and belted for those high trippin' days
of makin' it cool on Bleecker, at the Fillmore, in Tompkins Square
Park: you were so busy, boy—busy boy—holding the center
of attention, our lives, the wildness of dreams dreaming
on dreams, fearing those centers that no one can hold.

When you left our lives, long before you left our lives,
for the great unaltered state of the normal kind, crossed
into un-strung-out hemispheres of blood and brood,
earth-gift of care and family connection, home of your own
making, at last—did you ever really believe it was yours?

We did, imagining you found, somewhere in yourself, while lost
out there to us, fled, in folds of forgetting, from the sparks
we struck to recall you: you were living that long departure
of which beginnings launch, that older dream, of ends
that draw us landward, to lights we spy from the sea.
But this world is barter and debt. Clamor and throng, it follows.

What strange colors were staining the sky, with the blood
full drained from your face, when those whose lives you'd created
and crowned found you and lost you at once? Your final blue turned
theirs then, to worry and wear with the world. And we, who'd known you
before, king of our craziness, lord of our laughter, come to imagine again.

We only pretend there are lessons, yet we make recognitions.
We hear their calling, recalling shadows of what remains to be seen:
the city, a time, our young lives on fire, streets that burned with becoming;
and the low spark of your high-heeled boots, their clatter, in long-loping,
conquering strides, once aflame with the ferocious flesh of your shining,
full flush on the avenue in your jacket and shades.

Ocean's End

Along the coastal Atlantic at summer's end
the Caribbean's hurricane mood looms
over the waters north to New York, the Cape
and beyond. The season's swells deliver you
from the human traffic toward the sun
while the locals remain to neighbor their brooding god.

In fishing villages, the perennial change
in weather forces trawlers and dredgers
to make less picturesque and more dangerous runs.
Carnival barkers break for higher ground.
A certain kind of homeless drifter scavenges
empty, windswept streets and beaches for the leavings
of the summer parade. And the shore folk gaze from
grassy dunes, walk the water's muddy, roiling edge
in bare feet, rolled cuffs, to regard their drifting spirits.

For inlanders, the seas are circus amusements
great, gentle idiots who balance children on laps
for fun and snapshot reminiscence, but sometimes
the tide's embrace grows dumbly tight, and even
in the frightened, clutching struggle of arms
snaps a neck, and the god appears a terrible thing.

Sea people know this. They live beside the behemoth
as grassland hunters must have slept beneath
the pulsing night: fathoming the rhythms and measuring
each day by the length of the heaving rests.
What moves their world moves among them, but apart.
When the creature rouses, in leviathan havoc
stirred to upset by whatever earthly ill
they know the cruel and human cost
will affirm inhuman nature.

In the west, where I live now, along the southern shores
the ocean's more Pacific air will stage
these seasonal dramas, but waves more often
break the shoreline tamely
with maybe a lion's circus roar for show
and the sky sits upon this broad expanse
as if to cap a sleeping Buddha with a gong.

Here the barren granular and liquid planes
may bleach from cast-off eyes in soft repose
all the social colors the will recalls
and the vast earthly loneliness of the elemental world
becomes a native sphere. For all of cathedral creation
vaulted in desire beyond what artificers know
the tug of first conception is the tide to where we go.

In my life, I have lived by oceans, and peering
seen the slow-sailed trend to the vanishing point
of every kind of craft the distance draws.
The water rests upon its roundness, curves
in the mind as the clear sky falls in place.
The blue green oils the uneven face;
the fish schools speed the way.
The Gulf and jet streams
stream over the farthest cold springs
to where failing human calculation
measures only the turning vague
of every hard and specific thing.

There a small round island rises
at the flooding verge of sight—
unmarked but by a central slope
of grass on shell white sand.
A lone palm stands
irradiant against the purple air.
Nothing moves, nothing sounds
in still winds above the noiseless splashes.

Then do we fly or dream we fly
fast over the speeding white caps
wrapped within a rush of silence
to what further lapless latitudes may flow?

Infinite Nocturne

I am 66, at a desk before a dark-lit window, in the deep of the night
in a Brooklyn apartment: music plays in endless loop: writing:
thirteen years ago, in a cabin on the California coast, after my father died:
and I knew I would die: conjured cold time: its fire: burning: the Zbruch River:
Galicia to Poland, Mac and Goldie, peasant children: in dire flight:
in the deep: in the night:

I listened, too, at a slant top desk, off Riverside Park: the pool of night:
imagining: loop unspooling: fire burning: now, then: half my life ago:
the end of loving: again: set her in the bathroom: while I wrote: a light
beneath the door between us: opening onto music: from the hearts of space:

"Comets tracing their lone parabolas of sorrow," I ended.
"Jupiter, soon to be a moon of Saturn, soon—"

Though, in truth, she'd thrown the light bulb
I'd unscrewed from the lamp, above the persistence
of her writing, so I could sleep, at the wall
above my pillowed head, freckled
now, with glass, flew back to Virginia: fled time:

forever: I see myself: hurt: again: hurt: my father
harder hurt: time's hurt: time hurts:
by his parents: the soil: history: horrible: history:
needs a push: past the past: pull of a new
world: New York: all his life, then: loved: the new:

his father waiting: unspooling the thread: mother
waiting: who had not waited: those who never: loved the same:
receding before: the reaching after: new lives: old stars:
over Lewisohn Stadium the same stars: Rhapsody in Blue
on a summer's eve, and my father slept on a Central Park
bench beneath the vast Depression: wondering at the moon:
how it is the same moon that chased the boy: relentless:

through the tree space for sky: barren branches: up the hill they ran: Cossacks
coming: to be hidden: all your life from yourself: zayde Zakai, leading them:
home to safety: the boy, the girl: left behind: nothing but this photo:
checked the horses, sat and sighed: weight of an old Jew, younger than I:
peering, candle snuffed, askew through the window: the darkness:
thinking: the moon: the stars: how they are the same stars: which lives:
in the night: in the deep: endless loop: music from: hearts of

If I Were You

If I were you, what I would do
in the matter is what I would do
if the matter were mine
in which to do. Wouldn't you

if you were me, do as you would?
Isn't that the point of conjecture, to say,
lost in doubt about what may be good,
wisdom for you is to do it my way?

If I were you, we wouldn't be having this
conversation. I would be talking to myself.
If you were me, we wouldn't be having this
conversation. I would be talking to myself.

If I were you, tall and fair, and not myself,
short and square, saw through your eyes,
wore that disguise, why, I would then be you,
to which you might object. I know I would

if I were myself. But you have it all wrong, you protest—or I do;
it's rather to say, if I were in your shoes, so to speak:
standing there confounded, the future disarrayed,
these are the steps that I would take, the end that I would seek.

But If you were yourself, what good to learn from me
what I would do if I were you, or in your shoes,
when you can only do what you can do when you?
As for me, or I, why imagine you should be someone I can be?

If you were me, or I you, or whoever a pronoun will be,
you would still be you, I me. It's the law of identity,
the excluded middle, non-contradiction. It's not my place
to be in your place, as if we'd only one face.

If we were ourselves, always, integral and apart,
then let us become each other, we would still remain
another, beings in ourselves, forever different, a part
of something unspeakably separate and the same.

Ringolevio

Ringolevio, a children's game that may be played anywhere but which originates in the streets of New York City.[1]

It is played in the expanse of the day, in endless afternoon untethered from any dawn, until the free and heedless drift toward night, the shout and holler in the flowering air, dissolve in evening shadow.

"It's a game....played on the streets of New York, for as long as anyone can remember... There are no time limits, no intermissions, no substitutes...."[2]

Now, I cling to the absent day, embrace it missing in my dying arms. Attachment the Buddha said, is the root of suffering, though some translate *upadhi* as acquisition, so that acquisition is the root. I suffer the acquisition of attachment.

It seems likely that the game was brought over from the British Isles ... a game that is called Bedlams or Relievo... A similar game, called Prisoner's Base, was played by members of Lewis & Clark's Corps of Discovery against a group of Nez Perce.

My father's ring sat in the sun-browned flesh of a leathery finger, a black onyx imbroglio, set in gold, of Mars in profile. Nothing belonged to him longer, or to my memory of him.

On turning eighty-five, he passed the ring to me. "Do you want it? I'll give it to you," he said, knowing that what I wanted was not so much the ring, but the line it stretched between us.

There are two teams. In one version, one team goes off and hides. The other team counts to a predetermined number and then proceeds to search for the first team.

Romantic love and glamour inhabit us alike, I think, glamour a romance of the self, romance a glamour. They stream as moths to the radiant Next. Excite in its imminence. The cusp of coming: becoming. Glowing coals, exhaust themselves.

What is this fire—of the possessed or the possessor, pursued, pursuer, pursuit? My name was called. I heard it shimmer in its sounding, resounding in the expanding day, the deepening immanence: syllables separating
                                                                  in the currents.

Often, the game would go on so long that it was called on account of darkness.

Equal ends of a life. Beginnings and ends of a life. Forge in a fire. Weather and ruin. Iron wrought by the world's hard knowledge. Press. Impress. Mark and scar. Prevails what wound carried

so far, so that later work, greater work can be cast only in mold of the last. Fast, fix what world you know. Let not endings only their beginnings be. Make more of what follows than what was followed.

Anyone on the pursuing side can catch anyone on the pursued side by grabbing hold of them and chanting ...."Ringolevio, 1-2-3, 1-2-3, 1-2-3!"

The ring never fit. Sized, resized, still it slipped, slid, under whatever finger bore it. Wore it. Pocketed it. Forgot the pocket. Found it, fallen. Over again. When, finally ungripped and gone, I would not dwell. Thoughts only crush if you think them.

Jail is any confined area, a porch or stoop ... or a space between two parked cars or bushes where members of the pursued team are accumulated.

In the lurid light of memory lies a haunted cemetery of abandoned tombs.*
I open them and wake to live, find the death called love no longer love—in he no longer the one who loved—that leaves no body: old torments, untormented, sufferance of suffering unfulfilled, awful and of no interest now.

First thunderstorms, electrical, lightning storms, shatter the sky, strike the earth, illuminate this time in terror and wonder. What recover of wonder if terror had not taken time? Such awe. To be alive. In this world. Spark. Speculation. Lightning!

Any IN member of a team, can free all OUT team members in jail by barging into the jail without being caught, tagging the captives and shouting, "All in! All in! Free-all!" or "Home Free-all" in the Bronx.

The first time I played Ringolevio, I was seven years old. Fired with fear and play, we ran: thrill it was to hide oneself, and the danger in discovery. Assigned to keep the jail, between two cars on Hillside Avenue, I waited in my smallness for the raids I knew would come, to learn what comes of adding and subtracting,

to discover what remains.

Many corruptions ... have been concocted through the past century (not surprising, as the game's rules are passed by word of mouth from older to younger children).

Lift these words to the mottled sky to hold against its clearing.

---

1 Wikipedia entry on Ringolevio
2 *Ringolevio: A Life Played for Keeps,* by Emmett Grogan
* *Time Regained:* "a book is a great cemetery in which, for the most part, the names upon the tombs are effaced."

A Stone in Water

This stone.
This water flowing.
This flow of water
streaming over the stone.
You could look at it
all day
and never stop.
How the water
endlessly courses
liquid and bright.
How the stone lies
still below.
If only every day
could be this way
in stillness at the bottom
of motion
with substance at the center
of light.
You will try to hold it
in the palm you stretch
between the sediment and sun
just to believe you live
in the same transparent world;
you will hope to preserve
in the gladness of your senses
(like the blood running through you)
the same arresting motion.
But the instant
you always knew
was coming
arrives
succeeding like all the rest.
Now upon now upon now
the water flows
the stone stays still
and you offer your attention
knowing this moment, too
will last forever.

There Being

To arise
out of such that is
a darkness thus unknowable,
descend upon a thing so delivered,
a world alighted from within.
Nothing and everything
and all at once.
Neither nor each and every.
To enter time, taking space
in sudden slow passage through things.

To be becoming. Then to be.
Of someplace somewhere long before,
from some particular line of they
who like you, or not so thought,
remembered or forgotten, traveled
among the myriad drawn from then
to this.

How light
unshadowed across the face of it:
hills and towns, barns and buildings,
streets, still and motive, hearts at rest
or rapid beat, aflame with fire of it.
How summer sprang from it, seasoned,
sang. How, striving, fell into feral winter
or spirited the dark away. How love,
blossomed and broken, bore it.

Thrown from whence, to what, and why,
the slow sudden passage of things
that never were yours, nor time nor space.
Wonder at what it was that went, and where,
nothing and everything all at once,
to return again to such that is found
there, being.

www.ingramcontent.com/pod-product-compliance
Lightning Source LLC
LaVergne TN
LVHW041558070426
835507LV00011B/1174